CRIME SCENE INVESTIGATION

CLUES IN THE DNA

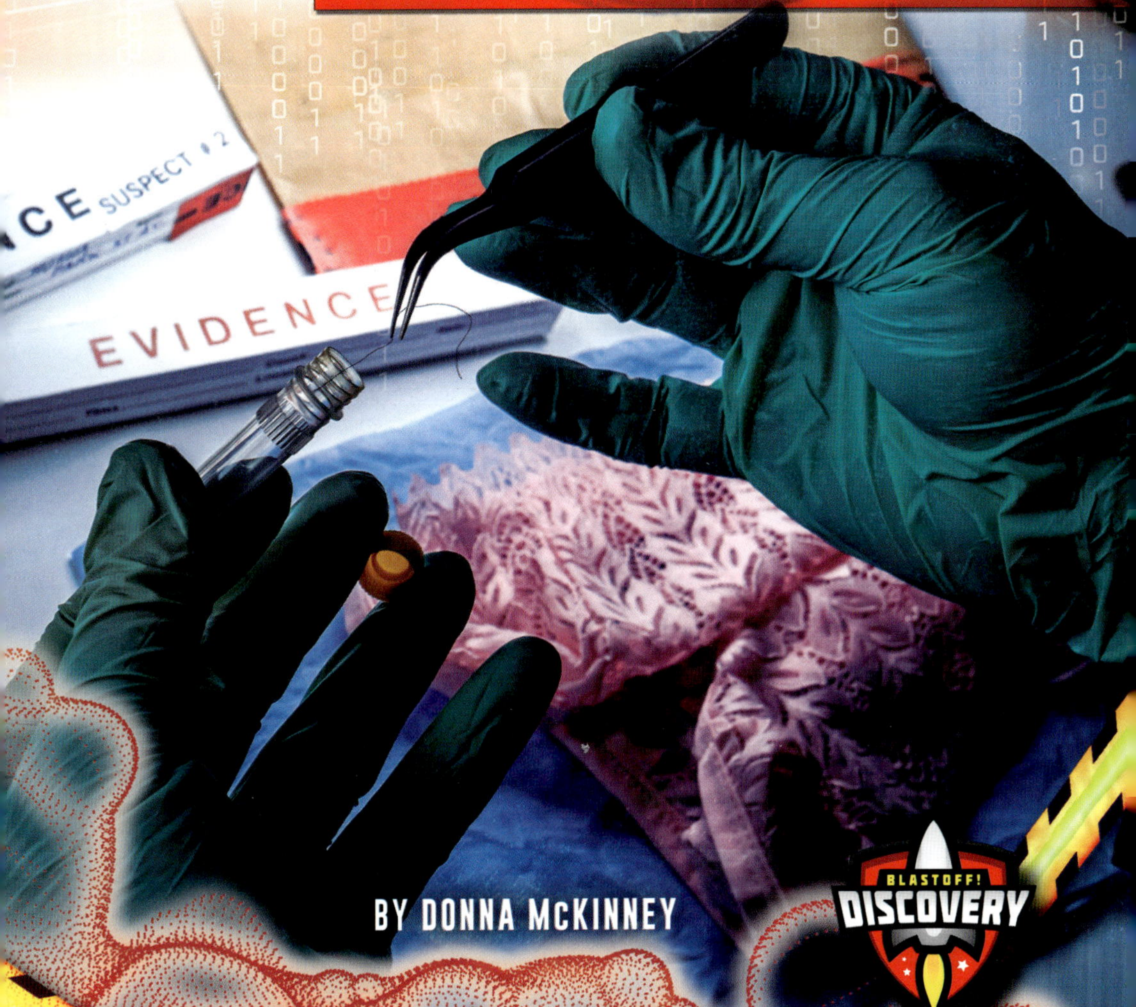

BY DONNA McKINNEY

BLASTOFF! DISCOVERY

ASTOFF! DISCOVERY, AN IMPRINT OF BELLWETHER MEDIA BY FLUTTERBEE

This edition first published in 2027 by Bellwether Media, Inc.

For information regarding permission, write to Bellwether Media, Inc., Attention: Permissions Department,
3500 American Blvd W, Suite 150, Bloomington, MN 55431.

Library of Congress Cataloging-in-Publication Data is available at www.loc.gov or upon request from the publisher.

ISBN: 9798898800802 (hardcover)
ISBN: 9798898802042 (ebook)

Editor: Rachael Barnes   Series Designer: Josh Brink

Printed in the United States of America, North Mankato, MN.

TABLE OF CONTENTS

WHAT IS DNA?

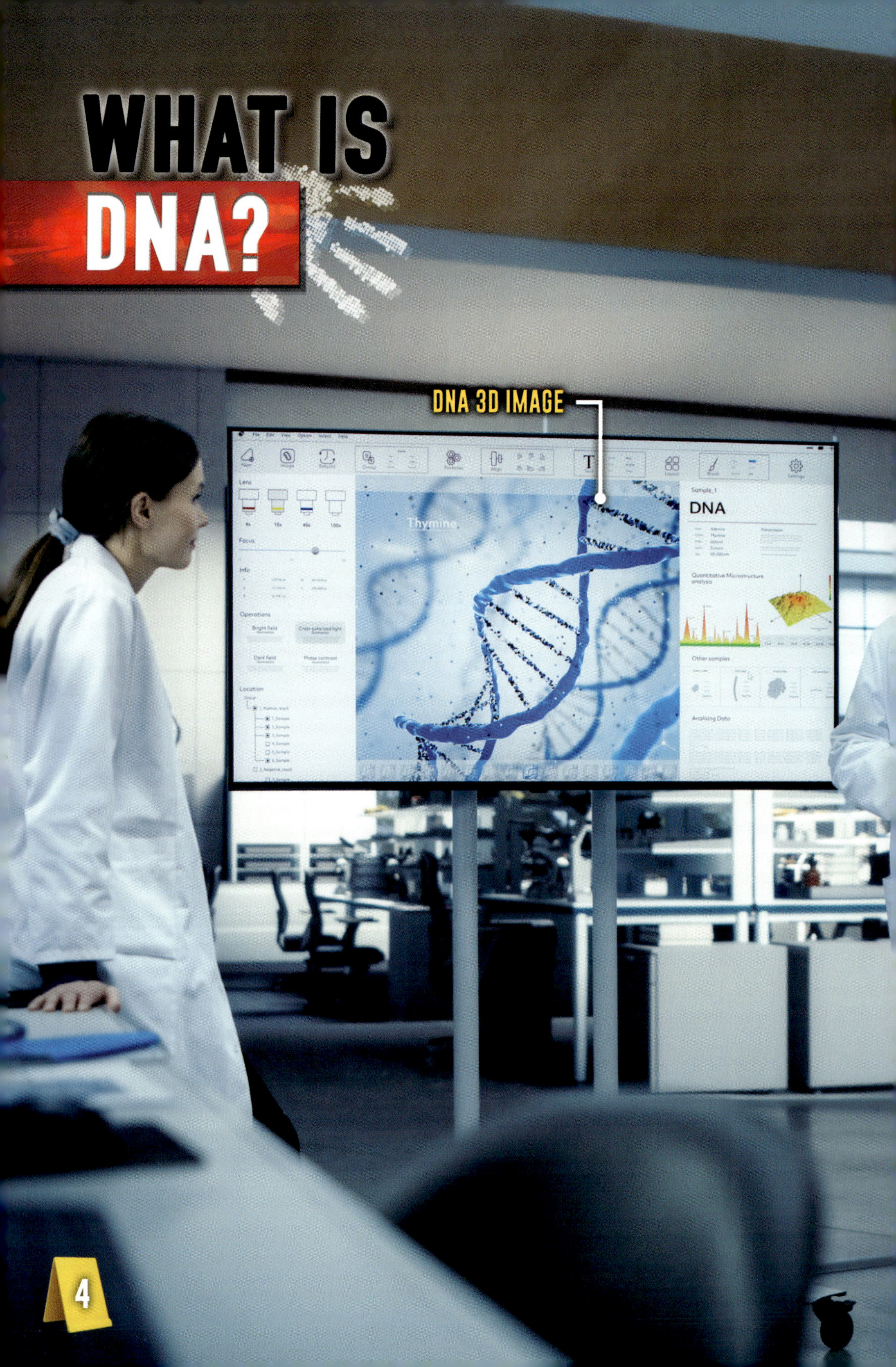

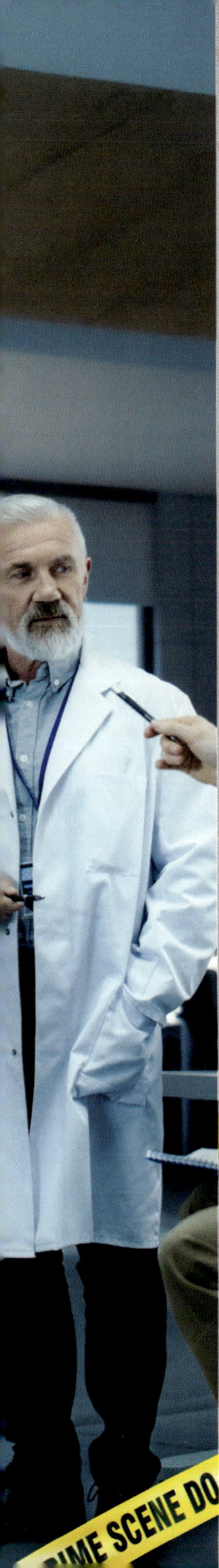

Every living thing on Earth is made up of **cells**! Cells contain DNA. DNA acts like instructions for the cells. In humans, DNA tells the body how to create organs. It decides eye color, height, and hair color. DNA makes people who they are.

It is hard to see DNA. Scientists must use strong **microscopes** to see it. They can also make **3D** images of DNA. These images help them study DNA better. Each person's DNA is different. This makes it useful in solving crimes.

NICKNAME

Some people call DNA the "blueprint for life."

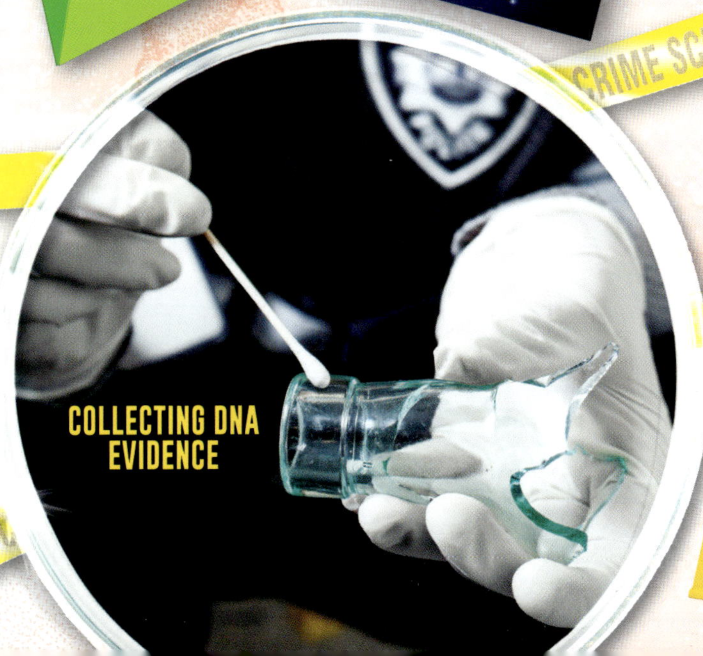

COLLECTING DNA EVIDENCE

SIR ALEC JEFFREYS

DNA was discovered in the late 1860s. Many scientists studied DNA to learn more about it. In 1984, Sir Alec Jeffreys learned that each person's DNA is unique. Soon after, Jeffreys helped in the first criminal case to use DNA testing.

At first, the study of DNA was called DNA fingerprinting. Today it is called DNA profiling or DNA testing. DNA profiling can help **convict** people of crimes. It can also help clear innocent people of crimes and get them out of prison.

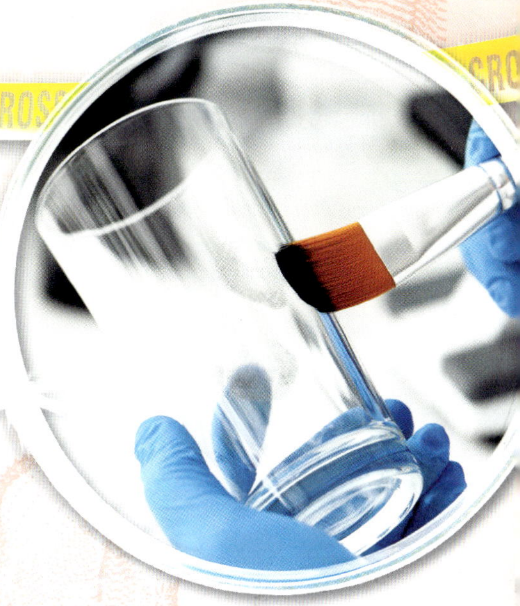

STATS

NUMBER OF PEOPLE RELEASED FROM PRISON WITH NEW DNA TESTS

over **600** people since 1989

NUMBER OF MURDERS THAT HAVE DNA EVIDENCE

less than **10 percent**

COST OF DNA TESTING

between **$5,000** and **$50,000** for one case

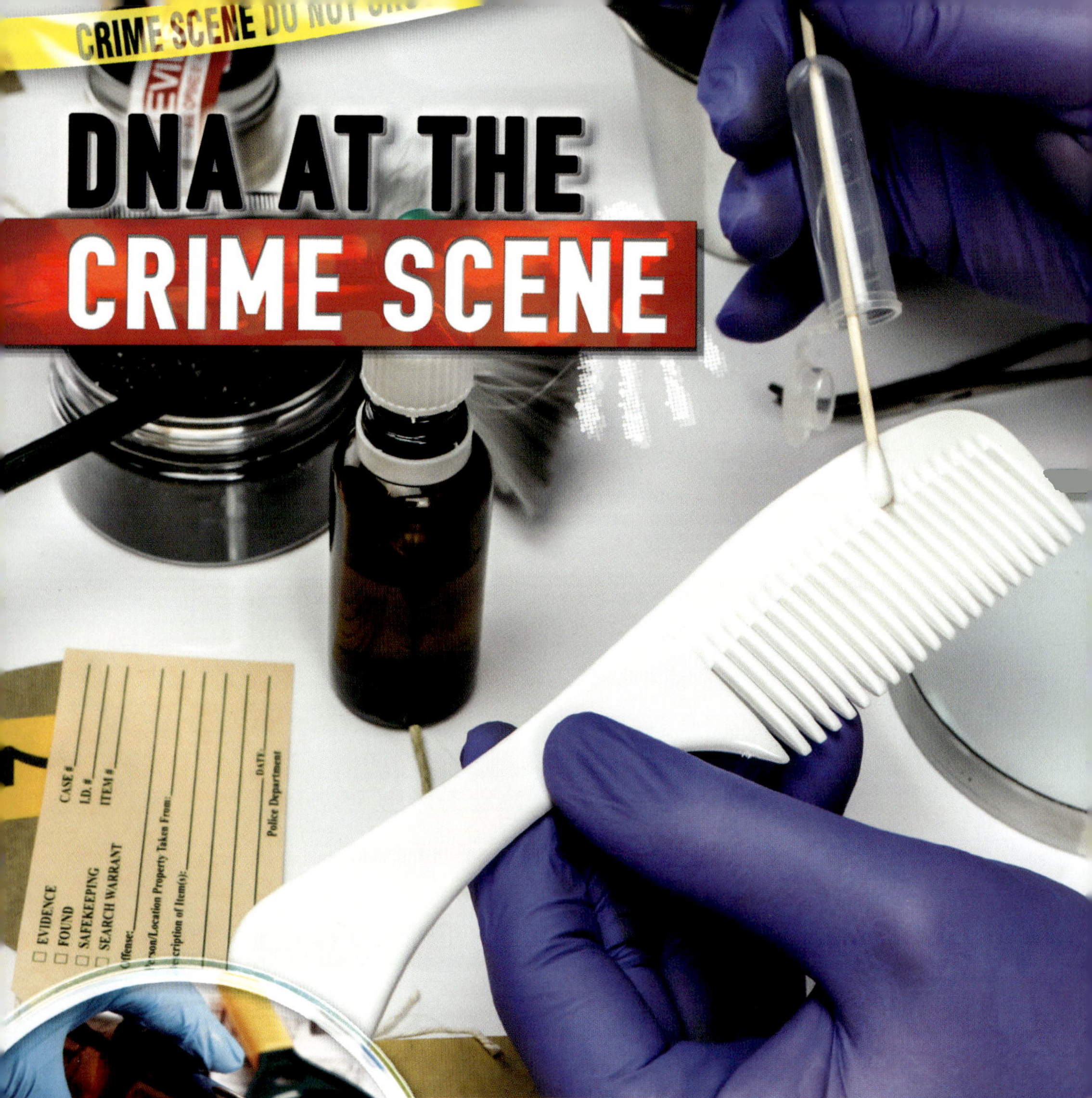

DNA AT THE CRIME SCENE

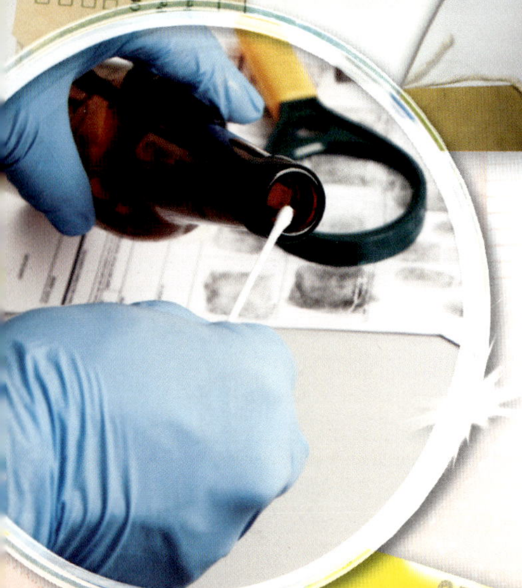

DNA is found in most parts of the human body. People can leave their DNA at crime scenes through blood, flakes of skin, saliva, and more. DNA can last for many years. It can be tested to solve new crimes and older unsolved cases.

CRIME SCENE DO NOT CROSS

Crime scene investigators (CSIs) collect DNA **evidence**. They work with police or on police teams. CSIs are careful not to **contaminate** the scene with their own DNA. CSIs wear gloves and shoe covers. They may wear protective gear such as masks or face shields and special clean suits.

CRIME SCENE INVESTIGATOR

HOW OLD?

The world's oldest known DNA is around two million years old!

CSIs can find DNA on any item touched by a person. This includes clothes, weapons, and cups. CSIs search the crime scene very carefully. They use different search patterns. Searching in a strip pattern is common. CSIs move back and forth across the scene in straight lines.

Sometimes CSIs start in the center of the crime scene. They search moving outward in a spiral pattern. Sometimes they search in a wheel pattern. They start in the center and move out like spokes on a wheel. These search patterns help them work carefully. They try to find as much evidence as possible.

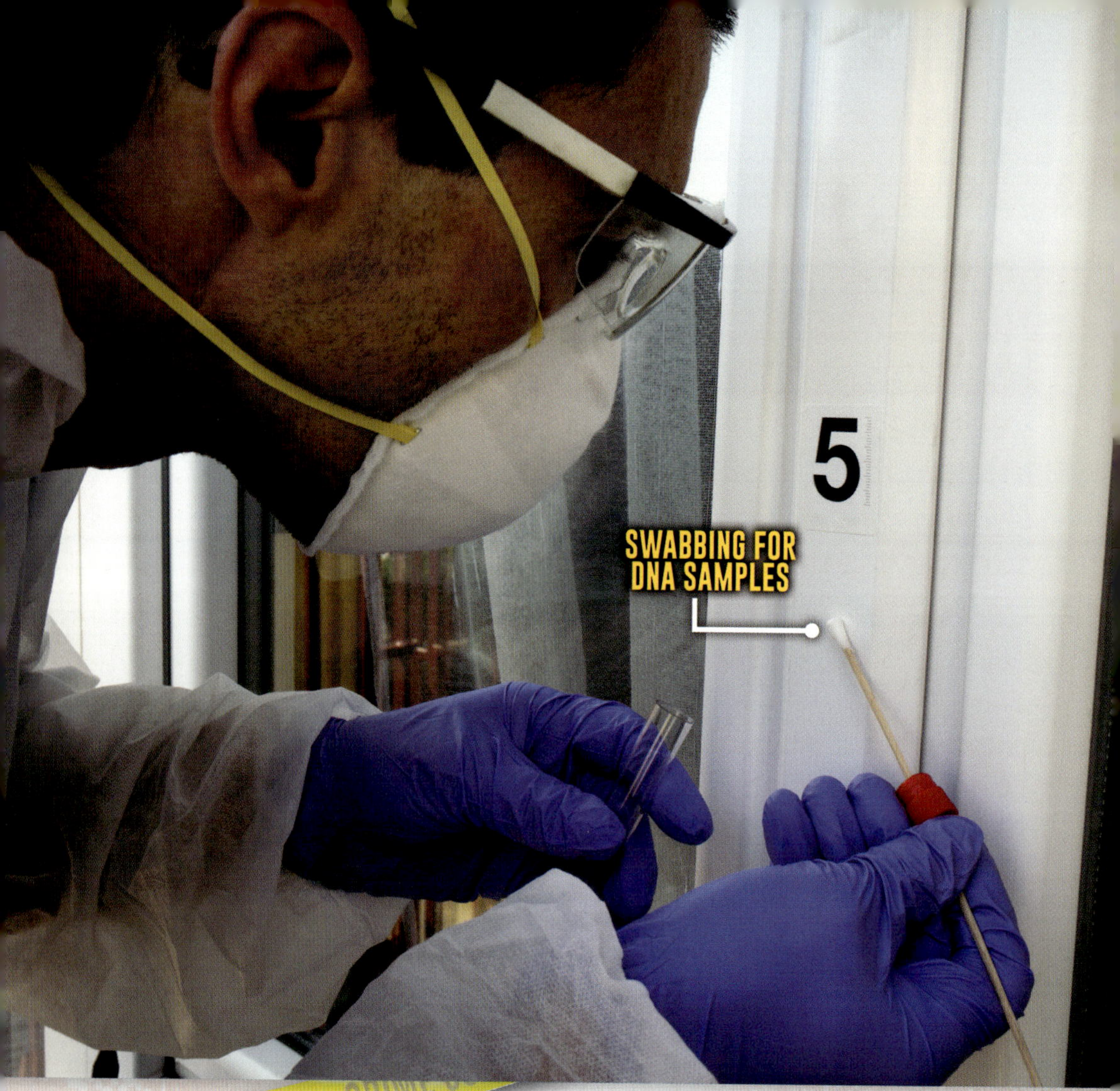

Sometimes the only DNA left at the crime scene is touch DNA. This is a tiny amount of DNA left when someone touches an object or surface. CSIs must carefully gather this DNA in different ways.

NO PLASTIC ALLOWED

CSIs do not place DNA evidence in plastic bags. Plastic bags hold moisture. This could damage the sample. Instead, they use paper products or other containers that let air through.

CSIs often pick up DNA evidence by swabbing surfaces with cotton swabs. They also cut to collect evidence. They cut a section from a stained item. Scraping is a method used for evidence such as soil or dried blood. CSIs use a clean razor blade to scrape the evidence.

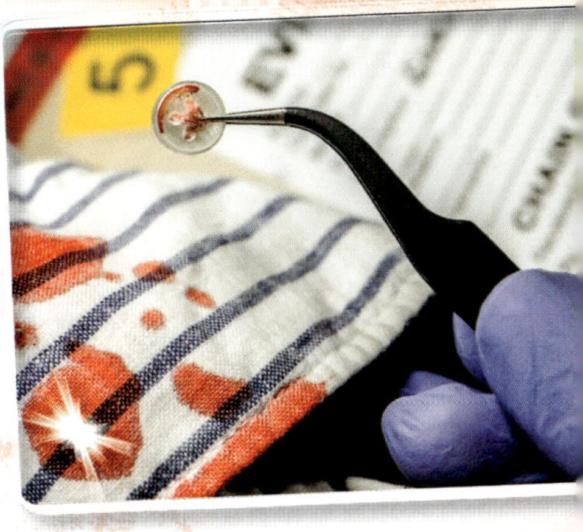

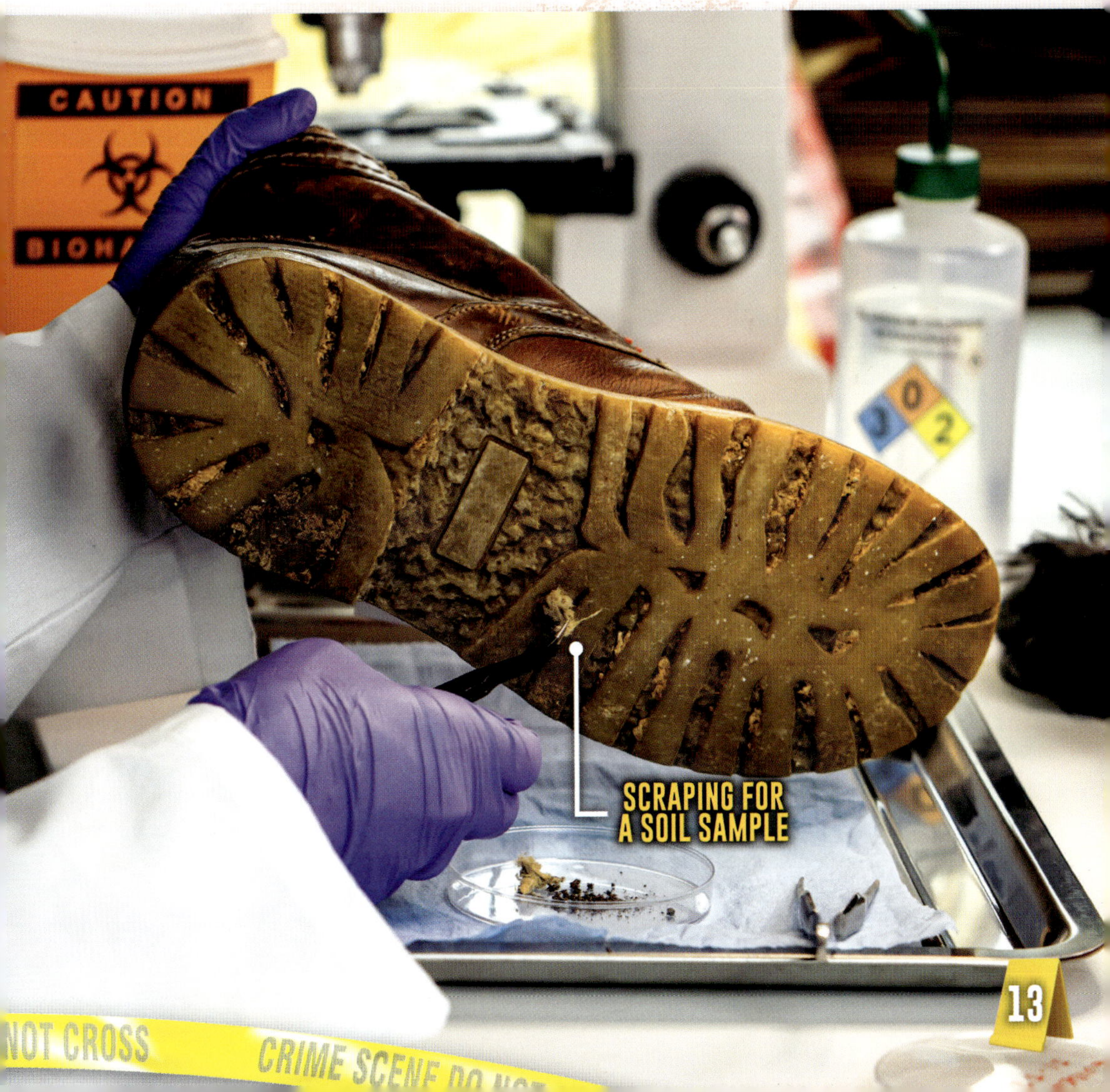

SCRAPING FOR A SOIL SAMPLE

Common items collected at the scene are fingernails, hair, toothpicks, and cigarettes. Small items that might hold DNA are placed in an envelope. CSIs seal the envelope with brightly colored tape. They carefully label each piece of evidence. The labels show the **chain of custody** as evidence moves from the crime scene to the **forensic laboratory**, or lab.

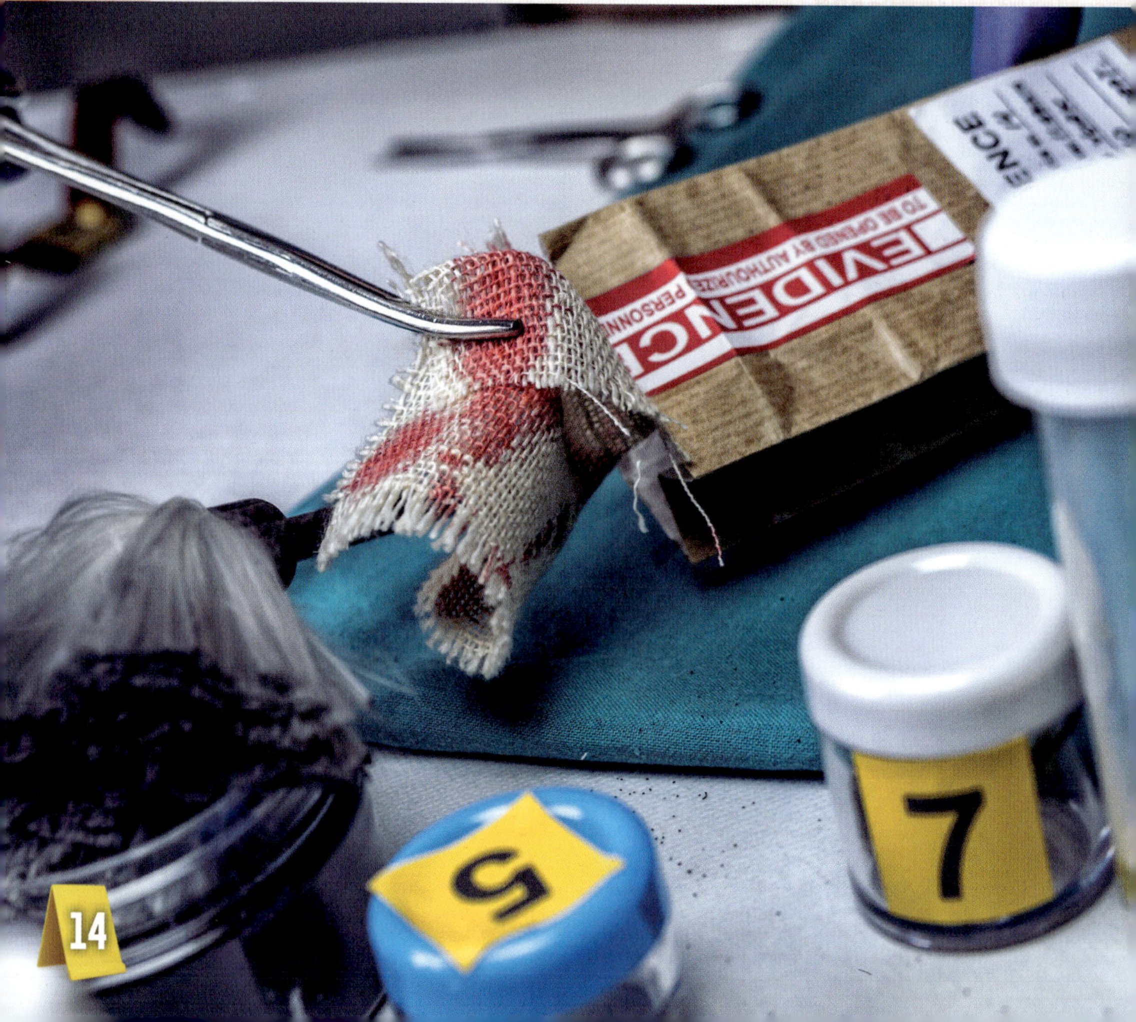

CSIs get DNA samples from people at the crime scene. This includes victims and **suspects**. They swab inside a person's cheek with a clean cotton swab to get the sample. These are called known samples.

RELATED BY DNA

Scientists can match family members with DNA. It can help people learn where their past family members came from.

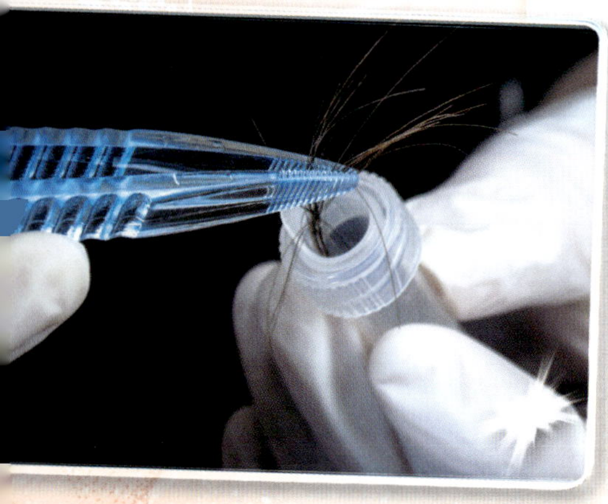

Sometimes CSIs collect elimination samples. These are samples from police and others working at the crime scene. These people are not suspects. But their DNA could be present at the scene.

Over time, investigation methods have become more precise. But this also means they pick up more DNA. This added DNA might have been there before the crime. For example, people leave DNA behind when they talk or sneeze. Touch DNA can make evidence **analysis** harder. It takes more time to determine which DNA is related to the crime.

DNA TESTING

CASE FILE

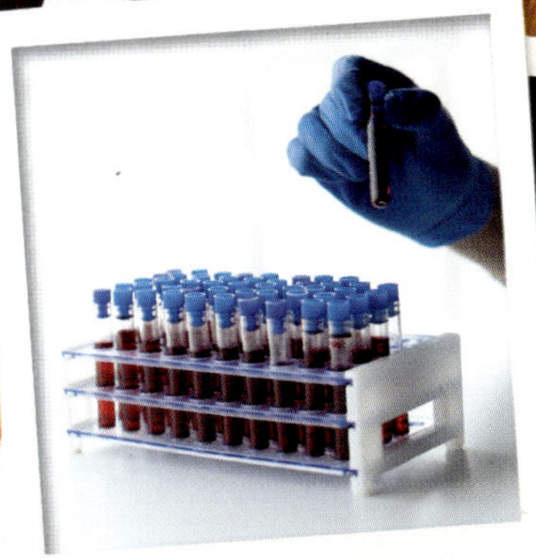

BLOOD SAMPLES

CRIME double murder and assault

YEAR OF THE CRIMES 1986

HOW THEY WERE SOLVED Investigators connected two murder and assault cases as committed by the same person. But they needed help finding the killer. Over 5,500 blood samples were collected. CSIs asked scientists to use DNA testing to compare the samples to the evidence in both cases. In 1987, they found a match. This was the first crime solved by DNA testing!

SOLVING THE CRIME

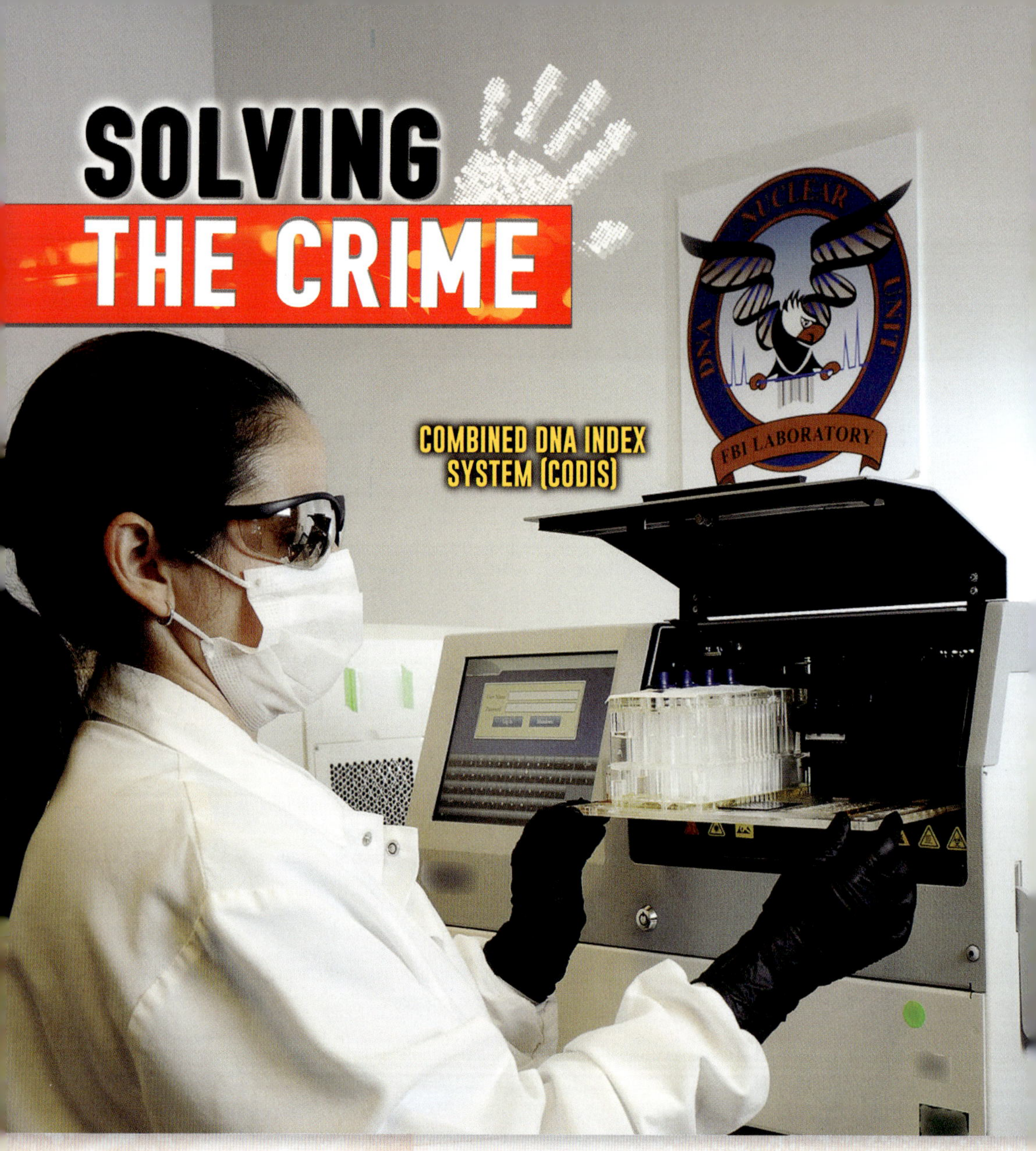

The DNA found at a crime scene is sent to a forensic lab. There, **forensic scientists** create **DNA profiles**. They use special machines to remove DNA from cells. Other machines make copies of the DNA and separate it into **DNA fragments**. Scientists use **sequencers** to read the DNA to find unique patterns.

They compare DNA profiles to known samples from the crime scene. They also compare profiles to the national DNA **database**. This database is the Combined DNA Index System (CODIS).

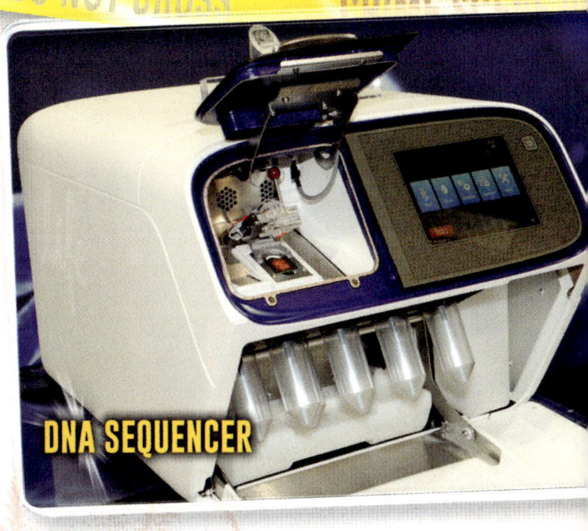

DNA SEQUENCER

COMBINED DNA INDEX SYSTEM (CODIS)

FIRST OFFICIAL YEAR IN USE

1998

HOW IT WORKS

Forensic labs use this database to share DNA profiles across all 50 states. Other countries also use CODIS. Labs can link profiles to people or unsolved cases in the database. In April 2021, the number of DNA profiles in CODIS passed 20 million!

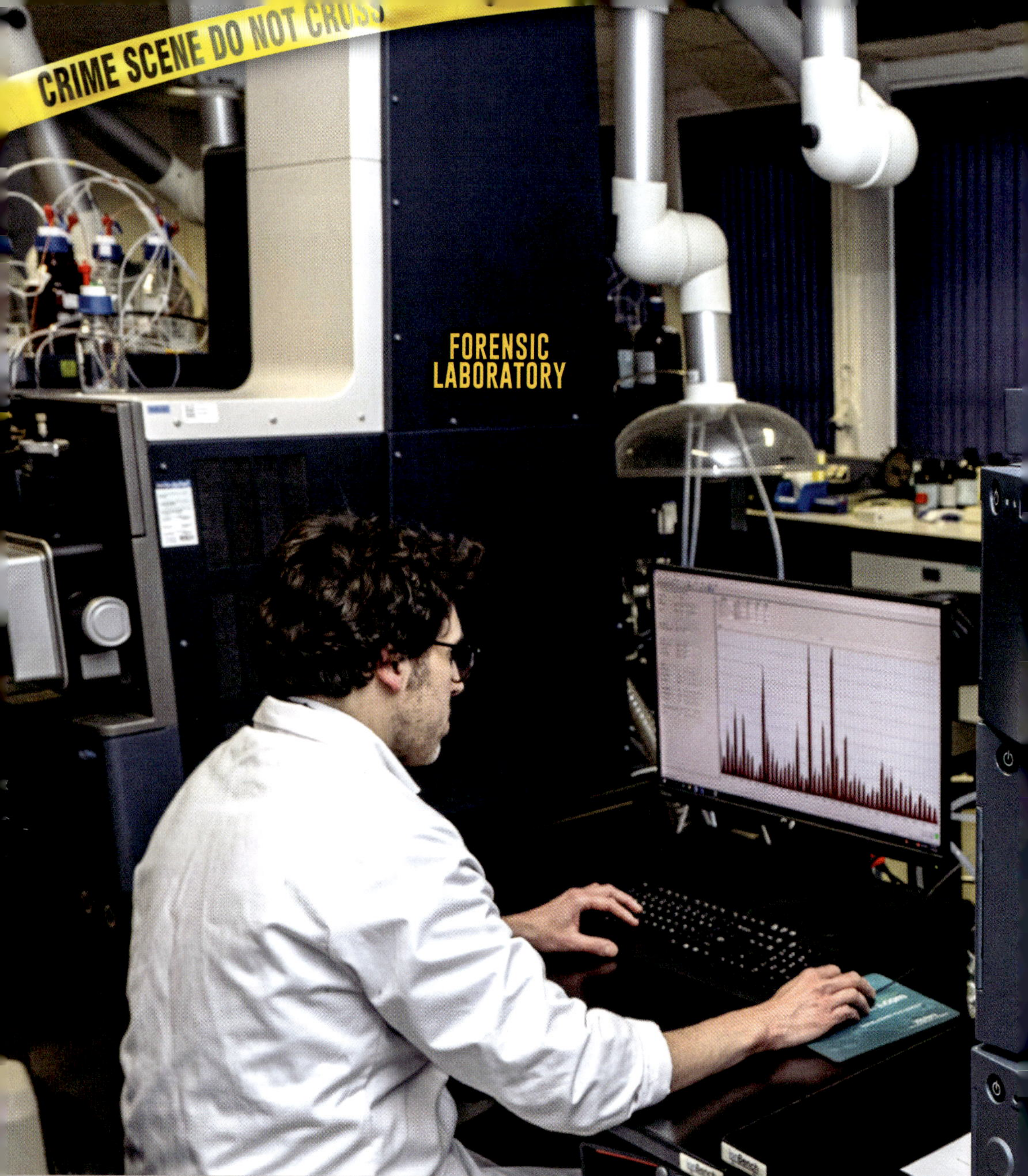

Human DNA is nearly the same from person to person. But some parts of every person's DNA have unique markers. The markers show the differences in the DNA from person to person. Scientists look for these markers to match DNA to crime scenes.

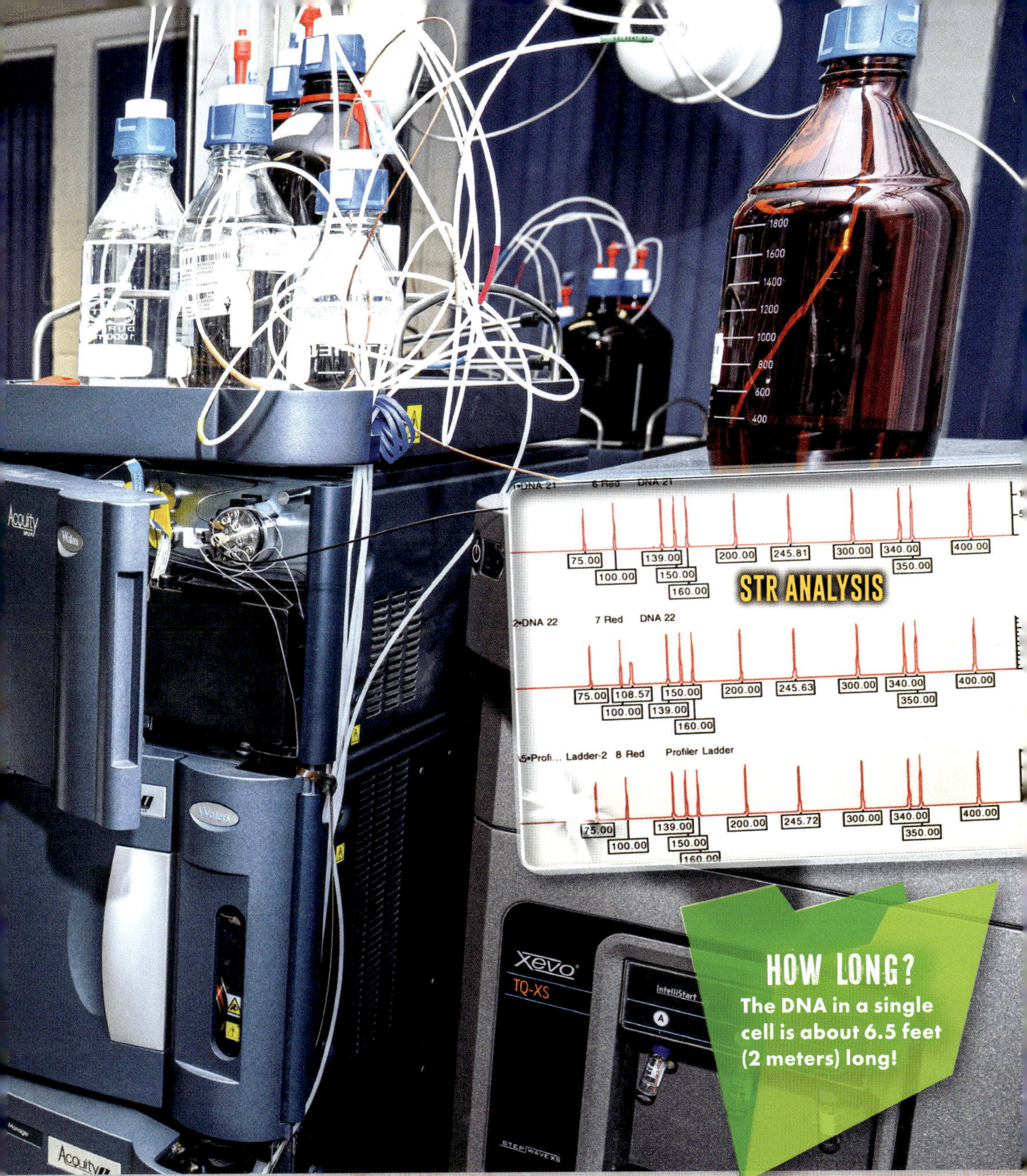

HOW LONG?

The DNA in a single cell is about 6.5 feet (2 meters) long!

Short tandem repeats (STRs) are one type of marker. STRs are small DNA fragments with repeating patterns. Each person's STRs are different. They are key to making DNA matches. Tests help find these small differences. Scientists read digital results from different machines.

Even when scientists are careful, mistakes can happen. DNA samples can be ruined. To prevent this, some scientists divide samples when they arrive in their lab. The backup samples let them conduct a fresh analysis if needed.

CHALLENGES

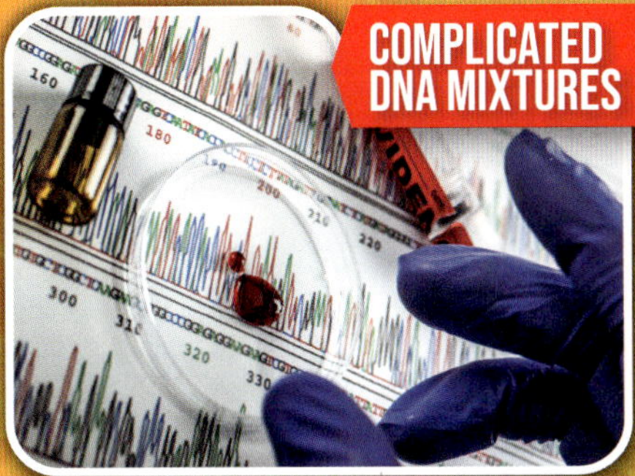

COMPLICATED DNA MIXTURES

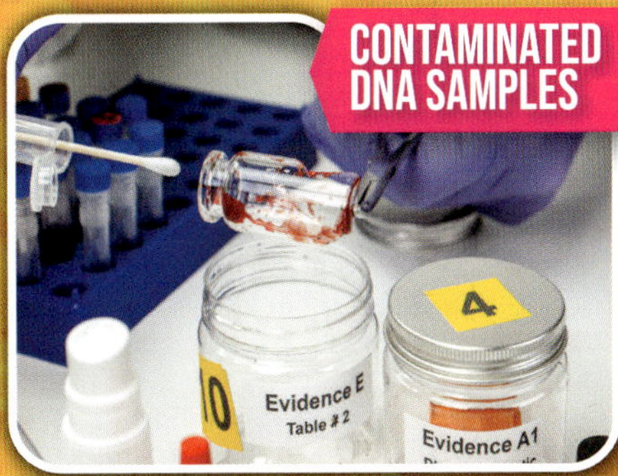

CONTAMINATED DNA SAMPLES

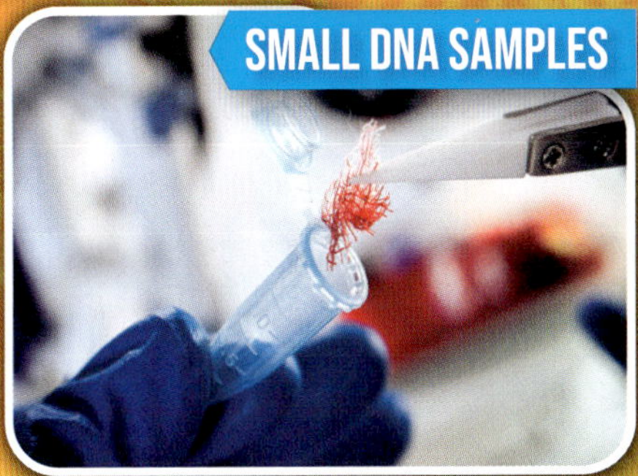

SMALL DNA SAMPLES

It can be difficult to profile DNA when multiple people's DNA is mixed at the crime scene. Scientists use computer programs to study complex mixtures. These tools help scientists solve crimes. In the past, these crimes could not have been solved.

Forensic scientists are often called to court as expert witnesses. They present their data. They explain how crime scene DNA compares to the suspect's DNA.

Lawyers on both sides use DNA along with other evidence and witness statements. One side tries to link the suspect to the victim and the crime scene with DNA evidence. The other side works to create doubt about the evidence. They question the lab results and chain of custody. A judge or jury hears all the evidence. They decide on a **verdict**. Even though it is rarely used on its own, DNA profiling plays an important part in many court cases.

THE FUTURE OF DNA PROFILING

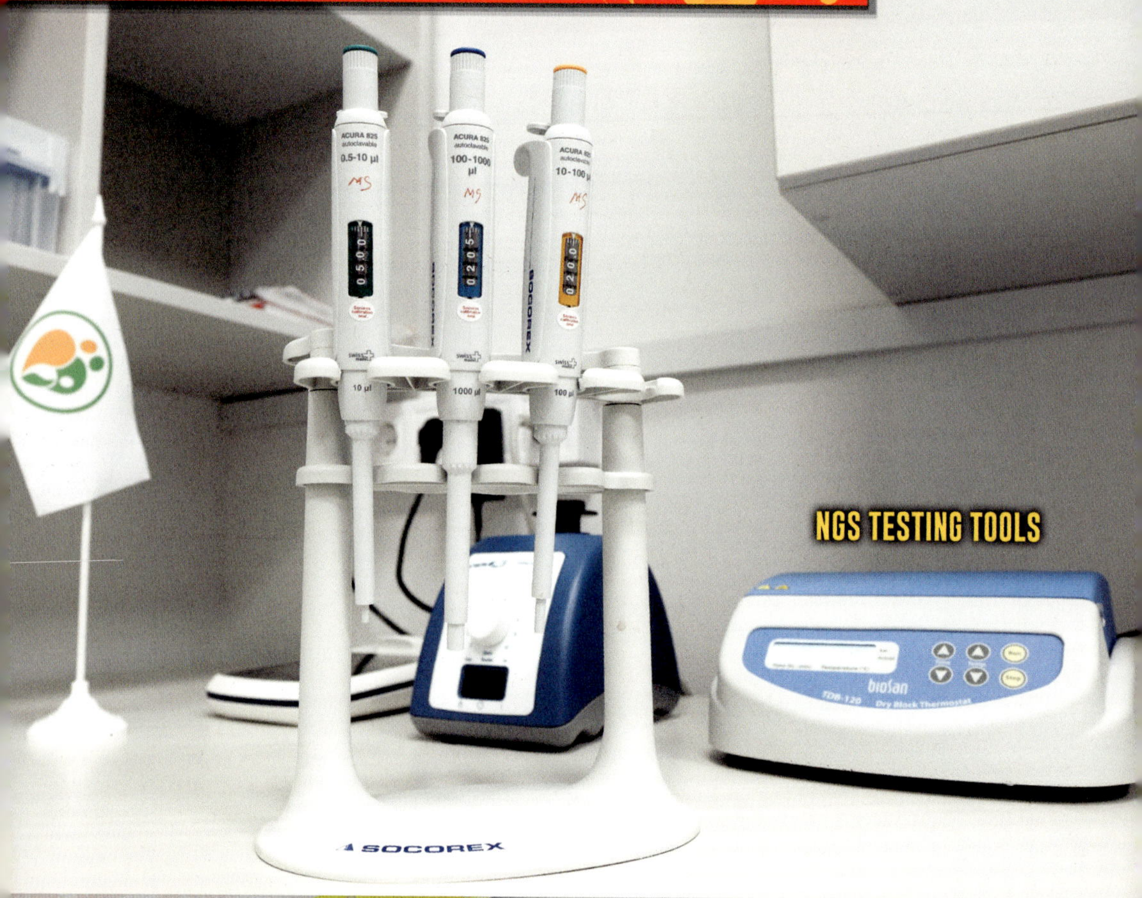

NGS TESTING TOOLS

Next-generation sequencing (NGS) is one of the latest technologies in DNA profiling. Earlier technologies sequenced just one DNA fragment at a time. NGS lets scientists quickly sequence millions of DNA fragments at the same time.

Artificial intelligence (AI) is also being applied in DNA analysis. AI tools find DNA patterns much faster than humans can. This is useful for working with complex samples. **CRISPR** is another emerging tool. CRISPR helps scientists achieve more accurate profiles, especially if the DNA is damaged.

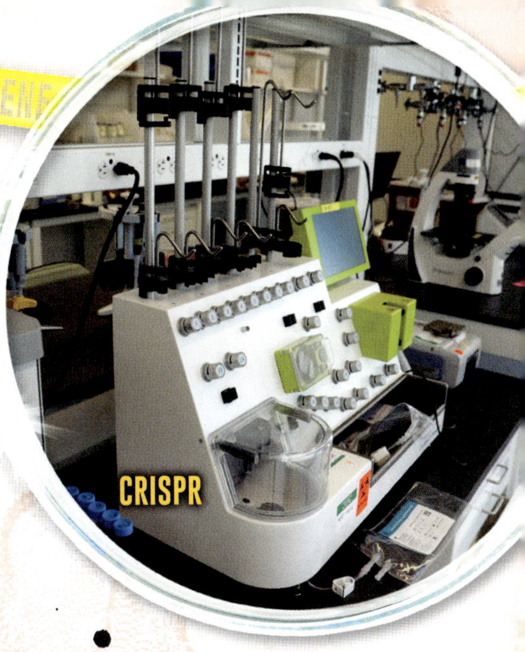

CRISPR

CASE FILE

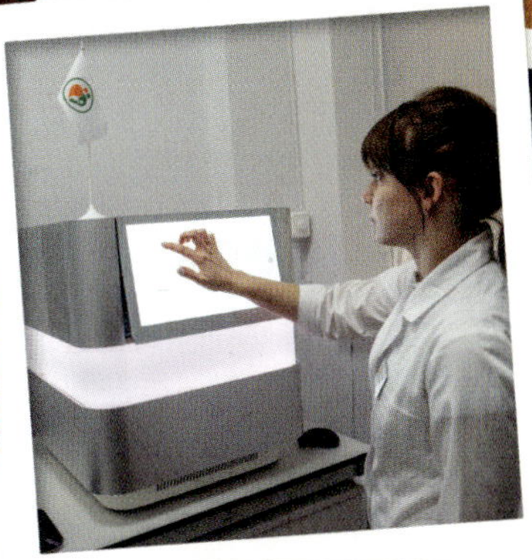

NGS TECHNOLOGY

CRIME double murder

YEARS OF THE CRIMES 2020–2021

HOW THEY WERE SOLVED DNA and fingerprint evidence were collected from two different crime scenes. NGS testing made it possible to determine the location and other details about the most recent murder. NGS was used for the first time in the jury trial. It helped convict the murderer in both cases!

CRIME SCENE DO NOT CROSS

DNA samples can be copied using PCR machines. These machines can make millions of copies from very small DNA samples. This method was invented in the mid-1980s. However, the machines are always improving. The latest machines allow scientists to test DNA samples that were too small to test in the past. Now they are usable.

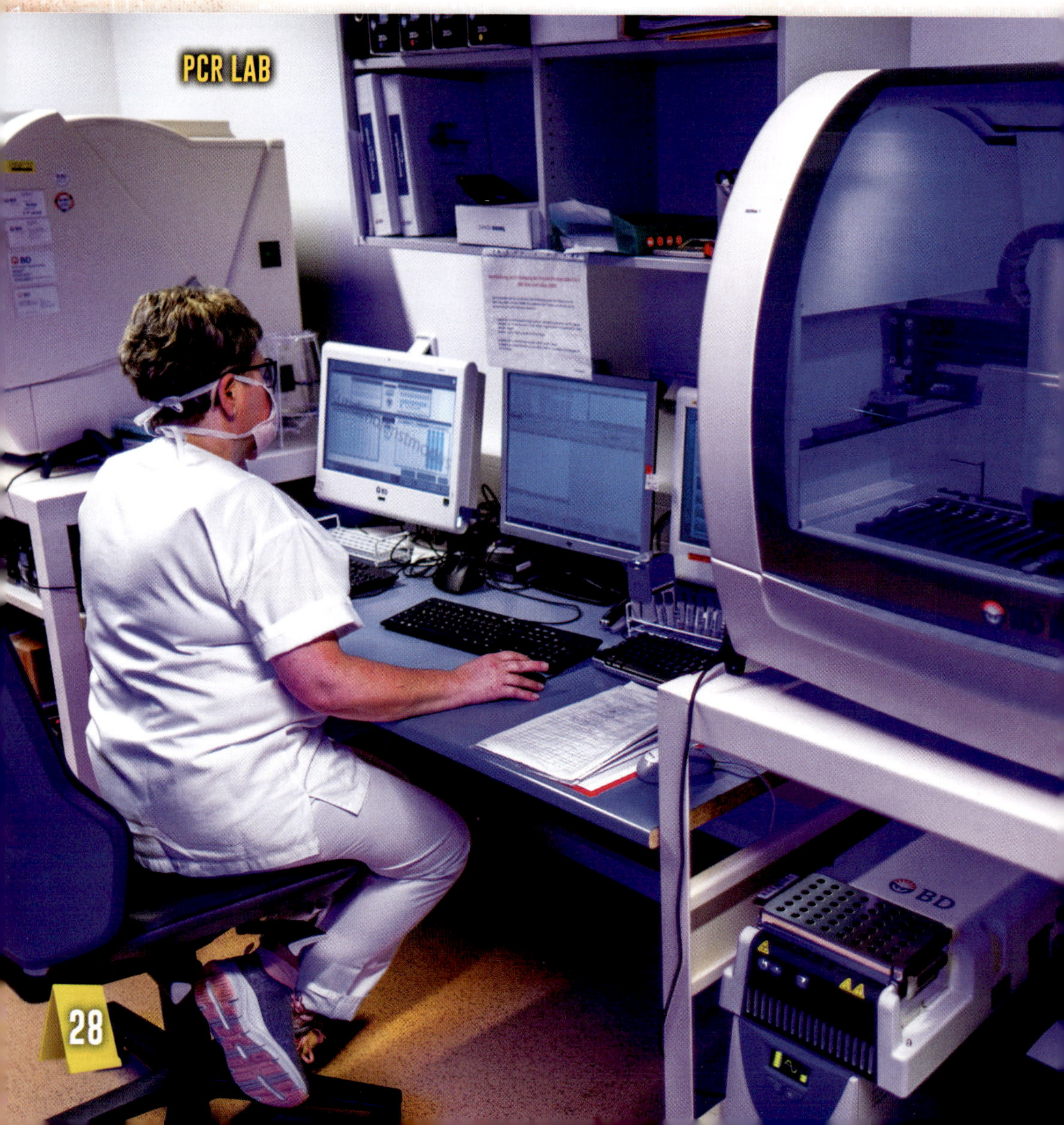

PCR LAB

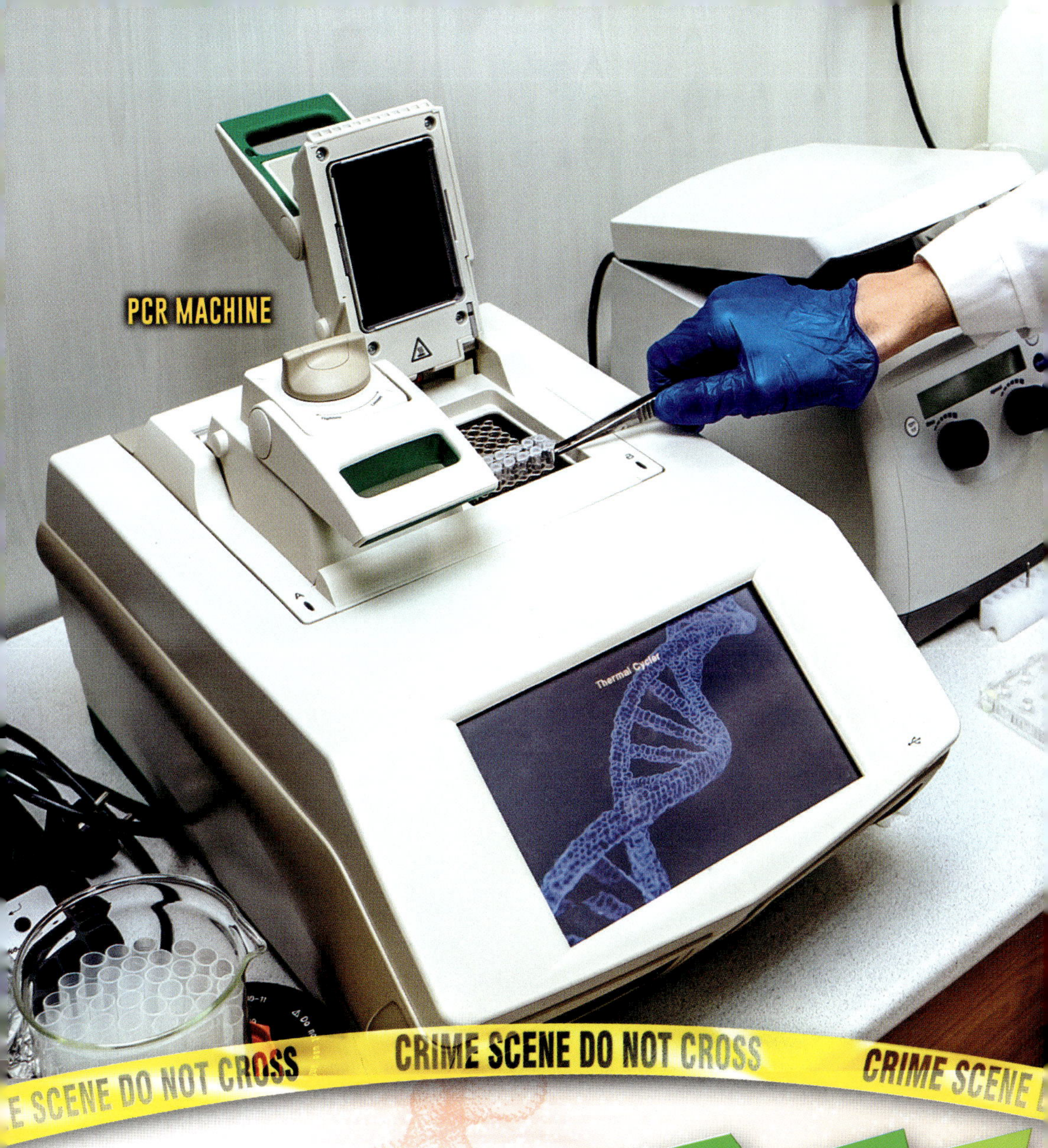

AI is now being used with PCR machines. These "smart PCR" systems get accurate results even faster. The future of DNA profiling comes with tools to continue catching criminals. Case closed!

IS AI FAIR?

Results from AI tools are still being tested. Scientists are working to be sure AI analysis is consistent and fair to use in court cases.

GLOSSARY

3D–three-dimensional; showing length, width, height, and depth.

analysis–the process of looking carefully at something to understand and identify its important parts

artificial intelligence–a computer's ability to do things a human mind can do

cells–tiny units that contain DNA and have different jobs in the body

chain of custody–the written record of everyone who handles a piece of evidence from the time it is collected until it goes to court

contaminate–to make something unfit to be used as evidence

convict–to find someone guilty of a crime

crime scene investigators–people who collect and analyze evidence found at crime scenes

CRISPR–a tool that lets scientists make precise changes to DNA in the lab; CRISPR stands for clustered regularly interspaced short palindromic repeats.

database–a digital system used to store and sort data

DNA fragments–small segments of DNA that are easy to test

DNA profiles–sets of DNA patterns or types that are unique to each person

evidence–a witness statement or an item or impression found at a crime scene that links a suspect to a crime

forensic laboratory–a place where scientists perform tests to study evidence left at a crime scene

forensic scientists–people who use scientific methods to study physical evidence

microscopes–laboratory tools that make tiny things look much bigger

sequencers–machines scientists use to determine the order of the four building blocks known as bases in a piece of DNA

suspects–people the police believe may have committed a crime

verdict–the guilty or not guilty decision reached by a judge or jury

CRIME SCENE DO NOT CROSS

TO LEARN MORE

AT THE LIBRARY

McKinney, Donna. *Fingerprint Forensics*. Minneapolis, Minn.: Bellwether Media, 2027.

Ross, Melissa. *Forensics for Kids: The Science and History of Crime Solving, with 21 Activities*. Chicago, Ill.: Chicago Review Press, 2022.

Woollard, Professor Alison, and Dr. Sophie Gilbert. *The DNA Book*. New York, N.Y.: DK Publishing, 2020.

ON THE WEB

FACTSURFER

Factsurfer.com gives you a safe, fun way to find more information.

1. Go to www.factsurfer.com.
2. Enter "clues in the DNA" into the search box and click 🔍.
3. Select your book cover to see a list of related content.

CRIME SCENE DO NOT CROSS

INDEX

The images in this book are reproduced through the courtesy of: digicomphoto, front cover, pp. 8, 13 (top), 13 (bottom), 14, 23 (challenges, all); Jeff McCollough, pp. 2 (evidence marker 1), 3 (evidence marker 3); Uri, p. 3 (evidence marker 2); Gorodenkoff, pp. 4-5, 9; Billion Photos, p. 5; anthonysp, p. 5; Homer Sykes/ Alamy Stock Photo, p. 6; H_Ko, p. 7 (top); Volodymyr Herasymchuk, p. 7 (stats top); Ground Picture, p. 7 (stats middle); PeopleImages, pp. 7 (stats bottom), 11 (bottom); Alisusha, p. 8 (bottom); D-Keine, p. 9 (bottom); Fiona Hanson - PA Images/ Getty Images, p. 10; WIKUS DE WET/ AFP/ Getty Images, p. 11; Zoka74, p. 12; andriano.cz, p. 14; Couperfield, p. 15; AB Forces News Collection/ Alamy Stock Photo, p. 16; SandraMatic, p. 16 (bottom); FBI media/ Federal Bureau of Investigation, pp. 17 (top), 18; PaeGAG, p. 17 (case file); Ethan Miller/ Getty Images, p. 19; Mikael Karlsson/ Alamy Stock Photo, p. 19; Belga/ Alamy Stock Photo, pp. 20-21; Streeter Photography/ Alamy Stock Photo, p. 21; Arne Dedert/ picture alliance/ Getty Images, p. 22; David Jones/ Alamy Stock Photo, p. 23; PNC/ Getty Images, pp. 24-25;. VINCE BUCCI/ AFP/ Getty Images, p. 24; Les Kasyanov/ Global Images Ukraine/ Getty Images, pp. 26, 27; Jonathan Wiggs/ The Boston Globe/ Getty Images, p. 27 (top); Jens Büttner/ picture alliance/ Getty Images, p. 28; Vladimir Mulder, p. 29.